DREAM CITY CINEMA

Books by Stephen Knight

Flowering Limbs (Bloodaxe Books, 1993)
The Sandfields Baudelaire (Smith/Doorstop Books, 1996)
Dream City Cinema (Bloodaxe Books, 1996)

DREAM
CITY
CINEMA

STEPHEN KNIGHT

BLOODAXE BOOKS

ISBN: 1 85224 376 7

First published 1996 by
Bloodaxe Books Ltd,
P.O. Box 1SN,
Newcastle upon Tyne NE99 1SN.

Bloodaxe Books Ltd acknowledges
the financial assistance of Northern Arts.

Cover printing by J. Thomson Colour Printers Ltd, Glasgow.

Printed in Great Britain by
Cromwell Press Ltd, Broughton Gifford, Melksham, Wiltshire.

for Katy Goodwin

Acknowledgements

Acknowledgements are due to the editors of the following publications in which some of these poems first appeared: *The Guardian, The Honest Ulsterman, London Magazine, London Review of Books, Lyrikvännen/Pequod* (Sweden), *The New Welsh Review, The Observer, Planet, Poetry Review, Poetry Wales, The Rialto, The Spectator, The Sunday Times, The Times Literary Supplement, Verse, Drawing Down the Moon: Poems and Stories* (Seren, 1995) and *New Writing 4* (British Council/Vintage, 1995).

'The Mermaid Tank' won the 1992 National Poetry Competition.

The author would like to thank the Arts Council of England for a Writers' Award in 1994.

Contents

like breath to someone else

The Big Parade

Here they come past High Street station, everyone I've ever known
and some I've only seen on television, marching three abreast,

my Junior School Headmistress at the front – Miss Morgan
with her bosoms now as much a shelf as when I saw her last

it must be thirty years ago – hurling to the sky a silver baton
(twirling up it tumbles earthwards like the prehistoric bone

in Kubrick's *2001*): turning at the Dizzy Angel Tattoo Studio
down Alexandra Road then into Orchard Street they go,

my other teachers – Grunter, Crow and Mister Piss on stilts –
juggle furry pencil-cases, worn board-dusters, power balls,

there's Adam West, his Batman outfit taut around his waist,
and then the Monkees, Mickey hammering a drum the others

blowing on kazoos: they navigate the Kingsway roundabout
to pass the Odeon where everyone is dropping ticker-tape

a storm of paper falls on Malcolm in a stripy tank-top, John
and Hugh and catches in the hairnet of our loony neighbour

Nestor – keeping up despite an ancient Zimmer frame –
and Bill the communist and Mister Shaddick, hirer of skips,

his brown bell-bottoms crack and snap around his platform shoes,
the collar of his paisley-patterned shirt's two giant set-squares

look! a girl from Pennsylvania who kissed me once, still thirteen
after twenty years, I shouldn't recognise her smile and yet I do,

I call to her but she's too far away, atop a jewelled elephant
she's waving to the crowd like someone fresh from outer space:

travelling along St Helen's Road towards the sea, the cheers,
the noises of the instruments resounding through the city centre

11

out, past vinyl three-piece suites and lava lamps in Eddershaws
go Mary Dorsett, Julie Dolphin, Tony (very much alive),

Rhiannon then a row of faces I can't put a name to now
but still I wave and shout and watch them disappear,

the boy who butted me one break-time skulking at the back,
the music fading, blurring with the gulls, the sea, the sounds

of people going home, till everywhere I look
the streets are quiet as a fall of snow.

Elvis

He's out there somewhere, in the dark –
a pair of oil-stained overalls,
a monkey wrench. When drivers park
to stretch their legs and scratch their balls

he appears with a chamois leather
in a pail of suds. He doesn't pass
the time of night, curse the weather
nor laugh; he only cleans the glass.

Bored, tired from counting off the states
they've spanned, they can't see how odd
he is, the man who never talks;

the tubby, balding guy who waits
for tips, then shrugs.
                                        The one who walks
across the forecourt like a god.

The Dying Seconds

Grey-faced & bald
the Number 12 is on his feet
again
running down the touchline
readying himself
His kit
is pressed
& every stud is clean
unworn
unused to grass

He calls the Ref
no end of names
or rifles through
the Physio's Bag
to smell
the sprays
the Magic Sponge

What crowd there is
is whistling for time
It's cold
It's dark
They've seen enough
to last their lives
They drift away
but all he wants
the Substitute
is bruises
phlegm
the taste
of mud

Then someone throws a toilet roll

Firs

The lackeys should speak simply,
without elegance.

− ANTON CHEKHOV

Blunt lipsticks, earrings,
Gloves but mostly hair,
Her discarded things
Wind up everywhere
I go: a bird's nest blocks
The sink while strands
Complicate each day
By stopping clocks
Or tangling my hands –
The strongest are grey
& wiry like mine,
The frailest blonde.
I should, I know, resign
& yet – too fond
Of her, contrite
When I have fussed –
I hold her lilac dress
Against the light;
Transfixed by dust,
In love with emptiness.

Orpheus

No smile no arms outstretched no kiss, only this:
The furbelows of rubbish on the escalator's edge.

The Day I Go,

preferably a Monday
far from anniversaries
& Christmas, may
the planet freeze
to its molten core
in grief – utter grief –
while strangers draw
breath in disbelief,
their voices trailing
as they mumble 'Why
oh why?', exhaling
with a cloudy sigh.

Well, failing that,
please, could the fool
who runs the bakery
next door find me –
my WELCOME mat
piled high with bills,
my corpse in bed
– then close his tills
& lose a single day
of trade; let his bread
rot, his ovens cool.
Then make him pray.

Daedalus

(for my father)

The sink is choked with dirty plates,
   Dead leaves, twigs – the tree
Outside the house disintegrates

   But Daedalus could be
No happier now he's begun
   To build his dream. To me

The watery autumnal sun
   Is cold and yet he sings
Out loud he's having so much fun.

   Obscured by coffee rings
& marmalade, his drawings flap
   Among the breakfast things

When breezes lap
   Doors and walls, our dripping tap.

.

Although he's working with antiques
   His father owned (the saw,
Flaked with liver spots, stalls & squeaks;

   The chisel fails to score
The softest wood; nails snap or fold)
   Still, shavings crust the floor

And clouds of sawdust fall like gold
   All afternoon: drifts grow
In saucepans. Sometimes, when that old

Paint-speckled radio
Beside the kettle plays a song
    He used to know

He sings along –
    Every other word is wrong!

                    .

He works all day, intent, absurd,
    Narrowing his eyes
Because his pencil marks have blurred

    ~~And~~ nothing's cut to size.
At sunset, when a sudden wind pours
    Through every room then dies

Away, he's there still, on all fours
    To improvise with string
& strips of Sellotape. Though doors

    Slam shut, though feathers cling
To him – his gluey hands, his hair,
    His clothes – he's whistling

Without a care.
    Feathers falling everywhere.

Ho Ho Ho

the elderly and ill
tucked up at last,
santa claus is still
gazing out, past
the mumbles road
towards the sea.
sleep begins to load
the nurses down.
an artificial tree
lights the floor.

in a white gown
at least one size
too big, he craves
the chance to slip
away.

      soft waves
crumble the shore.

medication dries
on his upper lip.

Young Siward

At break of day, the smallest bird
   (My second heart) beats its wings
Against my chest then settles down
     To sing.

At first, birds bearing twigs
   Alighted, now my armour fills
With song, song spills from every crack,
     Trills

Echoing for hours.
   I plait my beard with worms and leaves
Repeating   *crest*   *gorget*   *cuirass*
     Cuisse   *greave*

For comfort. Moss embraces me.
   The branches at my elbows bud.
Step by step, meadows turn
     To mud.

All day, beneath the drumming rain,
   I watch the black clouds block the light
Then march to Dunsinane;
     At night,

I dream of empty courtyards where
   Alarmed birds rise from me like smoke
And I am naked: frightened: streaked
     With albumen and yolk.

Last

We see The Straggler as often as it rains
                                    – skinny
hairless legs, a wheezing chest, dilapidated pumps
and blue cross-country kit –
                              stopping for directions
at the supermarkets built since he began

'Who changed the roads?'
                          'Who moved the park?'
'I could have sworn
                    this was the way'
                                      Perplexed
he staggers off
                through drifts of leaves or snow
forbidden to catch a bus
                          or – if he knew of any –
follow short cuts back to school

                              Weeds breaking
through the playground
                        crack by crack
                                        the names
on every desk long gone
                          his blazer alone
hangs from a peg
                  in the draughty changing room

horologagnosia

The Music of the Spheres

Sing a song of crow's feet,
of spectacles and Steradent

    of blistered paint, of brittle leaves
    while rattling a light bulb

        harmonise with headless dolls
        and broken spines of paperbacks

or, rallentando, jingle change
in pockets that are losing it

    sing a song of cobwebbed socks,
    of laughter-lines and liver spots

        join in with faded furniture,
        praise dirt around the light-switch

serenade the stars with dust,
with flowers stooping from a vase

    or croon a phrase that echoes in
    the hole where Richmond ice rink was

        sing a song of black snow
        and hymn the peeling heels of shoes

for everything that wears away
hum, cantillate, chant, whistle, trill

    you know the tune.

Portmead Lullabies

(for Karl)

Unbandaging a Motown song
my brother's tape-recorder's
reels are turning in the dark,
are sending me to sleep:

my eyes close on the green
fluorescent eye that flickers
for the high notes like my heart:
it must be Smokey Robinson.

My blankets tucked in tight
(preventing me from slipping out
of 1969) I'm picking at
the ploughed field of my bed

while, downstairs, wind
is singing through the big
glass door that coats
the world outside with frost.

The Price Is Right

That boarding house
– beside a church
that shook its bells
and crumbled starlings
from the spire –
divided, sub-divided,
rationing its windows.
No women overnight.
No pets of any kind.
I memorised directions
to the fire escape
then watched the box –
Young Conservatives
swaying in time, singing
'String 'em up'
or Leslie Crowther
booming 'Come on down!
The Price is Right!'
My personal effects
ranged along the desk
like booby prizes:
a can of Charm
for cooking smells,
a nest of biscuits,
pocketfuls of change
a meter by the bed
consumed. Evenings
in my claustral room
I'd stand alone,
before the mirror
above the sink,
to masturbate.
Cobwebs of semen
lolled in the plughole.
The water snored
away, the plumbing
gargled underfoot
(a minute, two)
then left that place
          in peace.

Before Evaporating

Pollution leaves a tidemark on the window-ledge,
the summer months it neaps towards the mantelpiece.
Perhaps the wood was grey when we moved in?

We haven't slept between the sheets for weeks –
your head is hotter than my hand is hotter than your leg.
Trouserless and flushed, I waste each day with words

or run cold baths, then soak until I shiver:
my footprints never wait for me to leave the room
before evaporating, so I sign the mantelpiece.

While – two doors down – the compère of a pub quiz
reels his answers off, I'm petulant again tonight.
The New York Herald. Roger Moore. The M18.

If only I had listened for the questions!

Cotton Wool

My Austrian grandmother died
   when I was twelve: although
a nun absolved her, she'd strayed
   from The Church years before.

Miles and miles away, my mother
   drank gin and whisky and howled
herself to sleep while I, I packed
   my ears with cotton wool.

Neverland

When anything bigger than a car roars past
our four rooms fibrillate: the glass in windows,
fish, the bed, the biro in my hand, my head.
Look at the floor – on summery afternoons
sunlight skirts the three walls like a picador.
No carpet is spared, no photograph untouched.
While jumbos from Heathrow buzz the building
flies bounce from A to B – I'm ready to go
with a rolled up *Richmond Guardian*.
Where Twickenham turns into Strawberry Hill
we've crept among the money like a pair of ticks.

Booming voices, rugby jerseys, differences,
at night the locals spill outside the Albert –
pub bands drown them out one Saturday in four
with love songs taken at a gallop and a shout.
The day you inscribed a copy of *Peter Pan*
Why can't we remain like this forever!?
didn't you think, like me, that we'd be rumbled
sooner or later? caught where we shouldn't be,
happy without a licence, at a lock-in
raising our glasses one last time and grinning,
with hardly a sound escaping to the street?

McAuliffe, Breath, Dream City Cinema & Leaves

Alerted by my exhalations
        bedbugs come
                to drink my blood

They track my breathing to its source
        then take fivefold
                their body weight

Every itch is something –
        flea larvae
                skip in the carpets
                skip in the carpets

thriving on the flakes of skin
        I'm shedding
                like confetti

'There is more life
        on me alone
                than people

on the planet,' you explain,
        while dust mites
                stop your mouth
                with crap

                ❦

A pigeon bleating in the chimney-breast,
Its beating wings creating falls of soot.

I look down at my blackened foot,
Consider getting dressed.

                ❦

Heroin trafficker Michael McAuliffe (38) of Queensland was hanged in a Malaysian jail last Friday. He had been waiting for books to arrive from the United States that he hoped would have taught him how to separate his mind from his body and float away from his condemned cell at Kajang Prison near Kuala Lumpur. His lawyer said McAuliffe had been desperate to live another week hoping The Magical State of Consciousness, Gateway to the Astral World *and* The Magic of Philosophy *might arrive.*

❦

Steel-shuttered
daubed with slogans
the corner shop was full
of bright ideas, labelling
the contents of its window
as a guard against amnesia –
Lovely Fruit Bowl
Cup & Saucer
Plate

Our barred
French windows
faced an unkempt garden:
once, I leant against the glass
sulking in a power cut
too proud to share
our one and only
candle

❦

Horologagnosia is revealed to the world in the latest Journal of Neurology, Neuroscience, and Psychiatry. *It means an impaired ability to tell the time.*

❦

His skeleton was in a chair
surrounded by Xmas decorations
from 1989. It was naked
apart from a pair of socks.

❦

34

I write
on anything to hand –
used envelopes, receipts,
the margins of *The Standard*;
I'm the one on the Tube
or the back of the bus
hunched up

(my biro
shuddering above
a leaflet for pizzas
or window cleaners)
regarding you
suspiciously

To judge me
by my cardigan
I could be a psycho –
nothing I write
is legible

Outside the house called Saskatoon
a disembowelled Vauxhall Astra
stains the pavement rainbow black.

Another Lottery roll-over week.
In Burgerillos, striplights flutter on –
moths mistake them for the moon

and while a mastiff draws its man
towards the verge on Ruskin Avenue
dusk covers everything like soil.

Every broken evening, drifting south,
blue aeroplanes display their tails.
British Airways. Alitalia. Qantas.

I dream of sailors
from the *Erebus*, unearthed
from the Arctic permafrost
(their hands against their sides,
their big toes tied together
with strips of cotton
in 1846)

and then
an old flame,
Marianne, who turns
like breath to someone else
before I say
'Hullo'

Curled on the sofa,
shivering, I rub my dead arm
back to life, laughing loudly
in a way I cannot
recognise

❦

Through a red door, a set of rickety stairs led to the first floor and recep-
tion. The stairways and banisters were wooden and fire was bound to
spread quickly. Cinema One had a 21-inch television screen on a stand.
At the back was a set of stairs leading to a balcony where sexual activity
took place. 'The average age was probably 40. Some were substantially
older. 60 plus. They fully participated if they got the chance,' said a
businessman. Ownership of the unlicensed cinema remained unclear yester-
day. 'There was a fat bloke there but nobody asked too many questions.'

❦

Warren – who has had enough –
tells the Desk Manager to 'stuff
£4 an hour' then throws
his headphones to the floor.
As he leaves, the glass door
shivers at his back.
                    Then he's gone.
A windswept E—— Street glows.

Name. Card number. Expiry date.
Inside, although it's late,
the operators carry on.

❦

Within the culture of late capitalism, dirt accumulates at points of production and consumption threatening the structure of economic and social relations.

❦

Leaves are filling the Fire Brigade's driveway

❦

I creep
from room to room
whispering 'Who's there?'
The white venetian blinds
light is breaking through
are strange: my hands
are also strange
to me

I find
saliva streaked
across my pillowcase
Numbers on the clock
An empty dressing-gown
The snaps of children
taken years ago
My shoes

Downstairs
I stare forever
at the pilot-light
'There's no one here'
I say, startling myself,
and then 'Was that the way
we used to laugh?'
to nobody

❦

the stored heat of the day
the neon stuttering

❦

I could burst
  and then
    I cut my skin
  and everything
is fine

❦

The dregs of office blocks
  returning home
    to snoring rooms
      & unlit wives
to carpets sharp with toys
  they haunt the concourse while
    a buggy courts
      the dossers with
a flashing amber light
  & spinning brushes
    sucking up
      the cartons
puddles, pigeon shit
  returning for a second bite
    of anything
      it's missed

❦

Alerted by my exhalations
  bedbugs come

through a red door

Hôtel Terminus

(for Sam)

The Rue de la Gare
                    vibrates like a bell
And shutters lose paint
                        Paint litters the floor

The sticky air glued (in folds) to my face,
Undressed, in the dark
                        I lie on my back
I lie on my side
                I lie on my chest

Mosquitoes arrive to dine on my legs

          .   .   .

I shower
          or pace the room like a ghost
Three steps to the basin
                        four to this bed
The mattress attempts to swallow me whole

          .   .   .

The waiting is worse
                    The stillness
                            The lull
Before I can cross the border of Sleep
The building erupts
                    and all Hell breaks loose

Deserting my side
                  impatient to leave
My passport, the key
                    my clothes and both shoes
Conga towards the door of this box...

The Land of Nod

even the dreadful martyrdom must run its course
Anyhow in a corner, some untidy spot
— W.H. AUDEN: 'Musée des Beaux Arts'

Waves shuffle up the beach
   deposit seven types of shit
then, chastened, slink away.
   Half-hearted spray
– more spit
than surf – attempts to reach

our esplanade
   but falls short.
As tired, as dim, we've stayed
   behind, acquiesced
in second best,
caught

cold, flapping
   our tails & clapping
our mouths in distress.
   We hug the shore.
We long for days before
this rusty mess.

   .   .   .

Outside MONROE'S
   a cardboard Marilyn
& *Every Nite is Talent Nite.*
   The blue, distorted din
of speakers grows
from dusk until first light.

Like other clubs
   cum renovated pubs,
this one heaves – bodies jar
   with everyone inside
lapping like a tide
against the bar.

Standing in our way
    bouncers deliquesce
behind their suits & ties.
    Instructed to say
'No' more often than 'Yes'
they narrow their eyes

but never blink.
    One word, 'Gracelands',
lets us thru. They draw
    a cross in purple ink
on the back of our hands
then open the door.

Inside, weighed down by gold
    – chains, bracelets, rings –
& lacquered quiffs, the Kings
    of Karaoke dress
like Elvis Presley to express
themselves: they're old

before their time: fat
    gyrating hips
& half-cocked upper lips
    murder *Wooden Heart*:
they stop & start:
they sound flat.

Bearded Elvis,
    Elvis with a stutter
– both eyes closed in bliss
    reaching for the notes – then
spangled Elvis in the gutter
smashed again.

Although they look a sight
    we listen to them sing
as if *Return to Sender*
    Lonesome Tonight
or *Love Me Tender*
meant everything.

Some nights, the moon
    above the bay (white
as any crimplene flares
    on show inside) stares
thru a skylight
while they croon

among the glasses.
    & someone passes
with a cloth, oblivious
    to all this fuss,
& someone senior still
counts out the till.

Ashtrays overflow
    with dust & cellophane
& furry beer-mats soak,
    disintegrate. In vain,
one bloke tells another bloke
it's time to go.

        .   .   .

The final Presleys out
    on stage (at last!) yawn
before the microphone,
    rub their eyes, then groan –
no one's there to shout.
Outside, it's dawn

and, returning to cars
    with smoke in our hair,
we breathe in the cold air.
    Beside the sequined waves
that full moon paves;
beneath the stars.

The Desert Inn

Sand is at the door,
Its progress through the keyhole slow:
I raise both hands to hold it back before

Sand inches, grain by grain, along the hallway floor:
Among the slippers, dunes begin to grow:
Sand is at the door

Of every cupboard, every drawer
Brims, postcards on the mantelpiece no longer show:
I raise both hands to hold it back before

My deepest rooms become extensions of the shore:
Now, where the goldfish used to come and go
Sand is: at the door,

In books, on pillows, more and more
Sand pours towards me: with one, whispered 'no'
I raise both hands to hold it back before

My waist, my chest, my neck, my jaw
And mouth succumb to sand, its undertow...
Sand is at the door...
I raise both hands to hold it back before

The Cinemas My Father Knew

I sometimes try their names aloud,
The Plaza
      The Tivoli
            The Albert Hall
imagining a post-war crowd
of soft-brimmed hats beneath a grey
October sky – a few
(in snazzy gabardines) smoking by a wall
outside the golden doors
                The queue
snakes a block or more away

my father somewhere near the back
as usual, with someone
              – not
my mother – dressed in black

I think it must have been like this:
facing front, they're holding hands
until
    bored of following the plot
(it's just The Bible after all)
              they kiss
and
    at THE END, everybody stands
for the King

      .   .   .

His old haunts burned
to cinders years ago – our coast
is studded with their shells – or turned
to bingo
　　　　　while in The Empire
　　　　　　　　　　　dust
constructs a thicker plush for seats
my father courted on –
　　　　　　　　　　the ghost
of Charlton Heston fleeing in disgust

Silence held in place with sheets

　　　　·　　　·　　　·

Since I was born, he hasn't been
or if he has
　　　　　he isn't telling
anyone

　　　　Staring at the screen
now, I think of him
　　　　　　　　back there
waiting for the Feature to begin

Stars going out
　　　　　　　Music swelling
and Moses

　　　　　stepping down to share
his pectorals!
　　　　　　　his brilliant skin!

After Lessons

The classrooms are as dead as winter trees.
You hold your breath along the corridor –
Your plimsolls creak. There is no other noise.

A single light ices the polished floor.
You turn and, somehow, end up in The Boys,
A row of basins level with your knees.

You shouldn't be inside this place so late.
I wonder what you thought you might achieve
By squinting at the blackboard. What, and how?

In the dark, you wipe your nose across your sleeve.
It's much too late to put your hand up now.
There's someone outside, waiting at the gate.

The Missing Years

My bedroom is fizzing with movement and light:
The window-sills, growing a layer of down,
Envelop the insects before I have yawned
And numerals purr on the digital clock,
They blur like the fruit on an arcade machine.
Dead bluebottles wrinkle: dead spiders curl up:
Whole weeks disappear before I have stirred,

Before I have gathered my clothes from the floor.
I watch every sunset explode like a match.
Despite the cold weather, my plants wave their arms.
Buds open to shed all their petals at once.
The soup in my vase will evaporate soon.
Alive and alarmed, hair springs from my face

While paintwork is turning to cobwebs and ash.
The bay window cakes: rain ploughs the glass clean:
Each moon (in a twinkling) is pared to the quick.
When time turns my stomach, I study my hands –
The veins, every crack – but the flecks in my nails

Career to the ends of my fingers and thumbs
Like fast-moving clouds. I study my hands
By day; in the evenings, the city is calm
Though traffic continues as rivers of light

And reams of skin swirl to the edge of my room.
In the middle of nowhere, the days pile up
While I lie still and watch this house decay.

Days topple into night like cigarettes.
With squares of light, the sun makes light of everything.

The blank-faced birthday cards. The black bananas.

Wake & Paine

The showrooms of the undertakers Wake & Paine

Are stranded here
                where Church Street turns to Water Lane

Tonight, and every night, one salesman will remain
Until the early hours

                    to breathe on every stain
The wood collects,
          to polish

                      Thick, autumnal rain
Hammers the roof with one, monotonous refrain

          .   .   .

(Stroking every coffin
                 one mourner tries, in vain,
To verify that he is here
                awake and sane

Another
      runs both hands along that polished grain

As though, by touching
              he could let his anguish drain

From every finger
          like so much rain)

The Mermaid Tank

Beneath my weight, the duckboards bow.
   Two buckets, slopping water, weigh me down.
A cold wind howls around the cages now,
   While rain sweeps in – across the town –
Again; and while our rheumy-eyed,
   Arthritic monsters fall asleep
     Or vegetate
      I kneel beside
The Songstress Of The Deep
   And wait.

All afternoon, the punters pass
   Her tank in single file; because it's dark
Inside, they press their faces to the glass.
   I breathe, at night, on every mark.
Behind my cloth, the water churns
   And curls around our fat dugong
     And when it clears
      (Like smoke) she turns
Away, and any song
   I hear

Is 'just the wind' or 'my mistake'...
   Outside, discarded handbills catch their wings
On tents or in the mud while, in their wake,
   Paper cups, ticket stubs and things
The rain dismantles every night
   Turn cartwheels in the foreign air
     Before they throng
      The sky, too light
To settle anywhere
   For long.

Yogi Meet & Deep

(for Paul Henry)

Tonight we leave our beds
To roam the jaundiced roads.
The street-lamps whine
And while our loved ones
Drool – through REM,
Downward to oblivion –

Afraid of sleep
We visit Yogi Meet & Deep.

The all-night stationer's
Accommodates insomniacs
In fleecy dressing-gowns.
Listen to our muted groans.
At five a.m. we are awake:
Tired of gawping at stars

Bored with counting sheep
We cannot sleep

While boxes of elastic bands
Bordering a central aisle
Stand like cardboard gods.
The worn assistant's hand
Cups our change: he smiles
Because his goods

Are plentiful and cheap
And yet we cannot sleep.

We bow towards the whisper
Of riffled slabs of paper;
In our nympholepsy, dip
Fingers to the second joint
In bowls of bulldog clips;
Or sniffle print.

Abashed we almost weep.
We long for sleep,

To dream of padded envelopes
 – Unposted, unaddressed –
Of unmade shopping lists
Of pots of ink, but it is late.
Now, along the chimney tops,
Look! a smudge of light

Begins to seep
Like sleep, like sleep.

The Surf Motel

Across the waves that vague, moss-covered knell
Drifting from The Surf Motel
's the dinner bell.

Starfish pack the car park at the height of every swell.

As always, every peal
Calls forth another conger eel
To nibble at the edges of the evening meal.

Silt and seaweed feast upon the carpets they conceal.

All evening, cleaners bail
Black water out of poky rooms to no avail –
Their patience and their buckets fail.

In hoover bags, like escapologists, fish flail

But still,
While tides will ruin everyone they fill,
Visitors remain for weeks, for years perhaps, until; until.

The cost of staying blurs on every bill.

the magical state of consciousness

The Rain

I dream of murderers
and burials and rain
the noise of rain
rain spattering the bed
drenched blankets
clinging to my legs:
in rooms my daughter
emigrated from
I search for dust:
I touch the tops of doors
the skirting boards:
the dents in every carpet
fill with rain:
and though the walls
are painted white
the pattern shows –
peering, I make out
lines of leaping fish
twisting in the air.
    I stay all night
I cannot wake
until, at five o'clock,
first light arrives
washing me ashore.
While the kettle boils
I read the postcards
on my fridge door
one more time.

The Flight Path

A friend of mine was hiding from his wife
behind the sofa while the room darkened.
Apart from one, bright red balloon
tied below his paunch he was naked.
HAPPY BIRTHDAY JUNE it said.
Plants and chairs were furred shapes
he moved around in silence,
bare feet slapping softly on the lino
as he thought how still it was,
how submarine. Along the mantelpiece
her cards had almost disappeared.
He tried to recollect the labradors,
the rosebuds painted with the mouth.
Radiators ticked like stilettos.
The black refrigerator purred.
A shiver rippled through him.
'It's nine o'clock,' he whispered
and held his breath to listen for her.
He felt his heart beating – then, above,
like surf, the faintest sound grew.
In the air a tremor bloomed, billowed
spanning miles in seconds, echoing
engulfing him until 'Christ not again!'
– his palms pressed on his ears –
their flimsy house shook: the glass
in every window whined, utensils
leapt from hooks and cups flamencoed.
Somewhere in the dark her cards collapsed.
Cradling his joke, his Big Surprise,
he looked around. The room was calm.
His feet were cold as blocks of stone.
    He thought about a safety pin.

Austria
(for H.L.K.)

The bed empty,
the sheets warm,
her one pillow
dented like snow.
While I apologise
to every nurse
for being late
the windows lay
starched light
on everything –
a thread of milk
between a jug
and cup forever:
a blanket holding
bell-shaped air
it won't let go:
the shiny floors:
the blank walls:
and, curled
like hands,
the shells
of tangerines.

Purity

A South Coast
sanitarian
her father
vets the tines
of every fork
but fails
to register
his daughter's
downy cheeks,
her bones.
She's leaving
like a cake
of soap
and all
he does
is simmer.
She drowns
his voice
with Blur
while mother
washes plates.
They squeal.
Downstairs
the napkin-rings
engraved
with all
their names
await;
the anguine
tails of letters
rising up
like steam.

The Landing Strip

On quiet days I furnish every room with food –
asparagus, blancmange, an ice-cream ingot,
a Marks & Spencer trifle served on china plates.
I cook for hours, the house is upside down:
dishes cake the floor, drawers brim with sweets.
I fill the sink with grapes, the bath with milk,
place knives and forks along the window-sills
then open every door and window wide.
I've no idea of numbers. One would do.
I listen for the sounds particular to them
– the different air about their massive wings,
the musical accompaniment, the choirs –
and wonder if they'll bring their instruments.
I watch for them: the light that shines
from every corner of their tallow hands,
their feet that walk an inch above the world,
their baby faces creased with baby smiles.
I know they'll smile. I've seen the photographs.
I touch the walls to feel my house tremble.
On quiet afternoons the weather enters, printing
blocks of sun that leave as soon as they come.
Or snow or leaves or rain-flecked winds
pour – like angry sprites – around the crockery.
Ice-cream puddles. Grapes begin to crack.

The Fire

Dreaming leaves
and breathing leaves
I circumnavigate
the white-walled House.
My breath is visible.
All day, leaves drift
to load the guttering,
leaves gather on the laps
of garden benches
and leaves are burying
the paths that lead
away from here.
I stamp my feet and clap.
Despite the morning air
the smell of burning
clings for hours.
   Unrecognised indoors,
afloat on long
somnambulistic afternoons
I follow handrails
down the floral corridors
and into rooms, to dust
those personal effects
I knew before I knew
their owners' names:
the hat and stick
on guard in number 3;
the handkerchief
that's folded twice
then left untouched
for days; the slab
of something sweet
by Mr Kipling;
the Get Well card
curled with age
and on the sill
in number 12
the yellow *Evening Post*

that published
scraps of diaries
and battle plans
disintegrates.
Miles from the Front
we warmed the bird
in a fire box,
on the engine
driver's shovel.
His grey arm
trembling
as he held it
steady

Near Wild Heaven

Waking to silence underground

among torn copies of *The Sun*
I see one other passenger –

his Walkman, his darkened raincoat

dripping, his brittle *A-Z*.
While rows of arm-rests glow

trains moan in other tunnels.

Time passes, drop by drop, and I
watch London fall to pieces

thinking I know the song.